REALLY WEIRD ANIMALS

FISH

CLARE HIBBERT

ARCTURUS

This edition first published in 2011 by Arcturus Publishing
Distributed by Black Rabbit Books
P.O. Box 3263
Mankato
Minnesota MN 56002

Series concept: Discovery Books Ltd, 2 College Street, Ludlow, Shropshire SY8 1AN,
www.discoverybooks.net

Managing editor: Paul Humphrey
Editor: Clare Hibbert
Design: sprout.uk.com
Picture researcher: Laura Durman

Library of Congress Cataloging-in-Publication Data

Hibbert, Clare, 1970-
  Fish / by Clare Hibbert.
      p. cm. -- (Really weird animals)
  Includes index.
  ISBN 978-1-84837-960-2 (library binding)
  1. Fishes--Juvenile literature. I. Title.
  QL617.2.H53 2012
  597--dc22

                        2011005601

Photo acknowledgments: Corbis: pp 9 (Ralph A Clevenger), 15 (Richard Herrmann/Visuals
Unlimited), 20 (Stuart Westmorland), 21t (Norbert Wu), 25 (Specialist Stock), 28t (David Wrobel/
Visuals Unlimited), 28b (Norbert Wu/Science Faction), 29 (Visuals Unlimited); FLPA: pp 5 (Birgitte
Wilms/Minden Pictures), 7b (Birgitte Wilms/Minden Pictures), 18 (ImageBroker), 19t (Ingo Arndt/
Minden Pictures), 19b (Gerard Lacz), 23 (Fred Bavendam), 26 (Reinhard Dirscherl); iStockphoto:
pp 7t (johnandersonphoto), 11 (cvdiver168), 14t (Rich Carey); NORFANZ Founding Parties: p 4
(Kerryn Parkinson); Oxford Scientific Films: p 16 (Paulo De Oliveira); Photoshot: pp 10b (Zafer
Kizilkaya), 22 (Charles Hood), 24 (Stephen Dalton), 27t (Reinhard Dirscherl); Science Photo
Library: p 17 (Christian Darkin); Shutterstock: pp 3 (Rich Carey), 6 (bierchen), 8 (bernd.neeser),
10t (Teguh Tirtaputra), 12t (Nikita Tiunov), 12b (Rich Carey), 13t (Rich Carey), 13b (stephan
kerkhofs), 14b (Rich Carey), 21b (tonobalaguerf), 27b (Joe Belanger), 31 (Teguh Tirtaputra), 32
(stephan kerkhofs); Ada Staal: cover and p 1.

Cover picture: A lionfish.

SL001751US
Supplier 04, Date 0411, Print Run 1055

Rosy-Lipped Batfish

Look at this glamour-puss! The rosy-lipped batfish isn't a good swimmer, but has modified fins that allow it to walk across the seabed. They make it look like it has legs!

WEIRD OR WHAT?

The batfish has a lure of frilly flesh on its forehead that tempts prey close enough to eat.

The fish's red "lipstick" helps other rosy-lipped batfish recognize it at spawning time.

ROSY-LIPPED BATFISH FACTS

SIZE: up to 14 in. long
HOME: off Cocos Island, Costa Rica
EATS: small fish, crustaceans
(shrimps, mollusks, crabs)

Frogfish

Frogfish live in warm, shallow seas. There are about 60 different species. Some blend in with the seabed and some with their colorful coral-reef surroundings.

WEIRD OR WHAT?

Some frogfish can change color to match their surroundings.

Like batfish, frogfish have leglike pectoral fins. They use these to crawl slowly across the seabed.

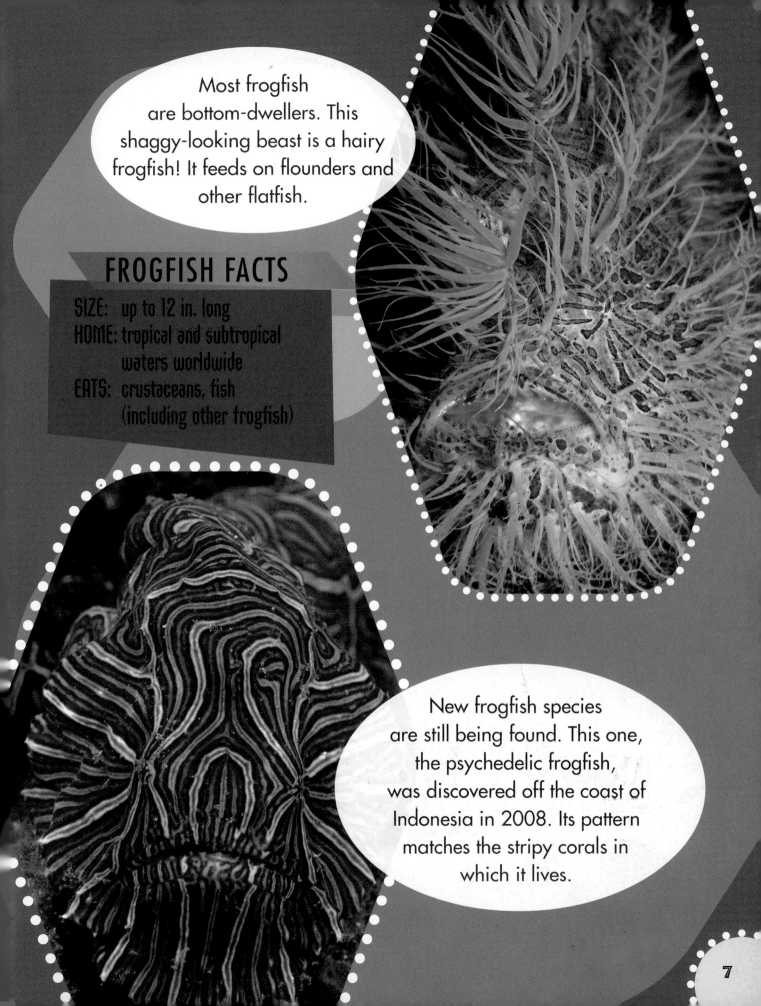

Most frogfish are bottom-dwellers. This shaggy-looking beast is a hairy frogfish! It feeds on flounders and other flatfish.

FROGFISH FACTS

SIZE: up to 12 in. long
HOME: tropical and subtropical waters worldwide
EATS: crustaceans, fish (including other frogfish)

New frogfish species are still being found. This one, the psychedelic frogfish, was discovered off the coast of Indonesia in 2008. Its pattern matches the stripy corals in which it lives.

STONEFISH

STONEFISH FACTS

SIZE: up to 14 in. long
HOME: shallow, tropical waters
of the Indo-Pacific
EATS: small fish, shrimps

Is it a piece of weed-covered rock, or a fish? Stonefish are disguised to look like stones lying on the seabed. This camouflage hides them from prey and predators, such as bottom-feeding sharks and rays.

Stonefish have another defense, too— a row of needle-like spines on their back that can inject deadly venom.

WEIRD OR WHAT?

Stonefish venom can kill a person within two hours—unless he or she is treated in time with antivenin.

This fish isn't called "sarcastic" because it makes harsh remarks. Sarcastic originally meant "tearing of flesh." Sarcastic fringeheads are certainly very aggressive. They defend their territory from other fringeheads by tussling with their mouths.

SARCASTIC FRINGEHEAD FACTS

SIZE: up to 12 in. long
(usually around 6 in.)
HOME: off the US Pacific coast
EATS: small crustaceans

SARCASTIC FRINGEHEAD

WEIRD OR WHAT?

If it can't find a rocky crevice, a sarcastic fringehead may set up home in an empty snail shell or even an old bottle!

The fringehead squashes itself into a crevice but pops out to ambush prey. The hidey-hole also protects its scaleless body.

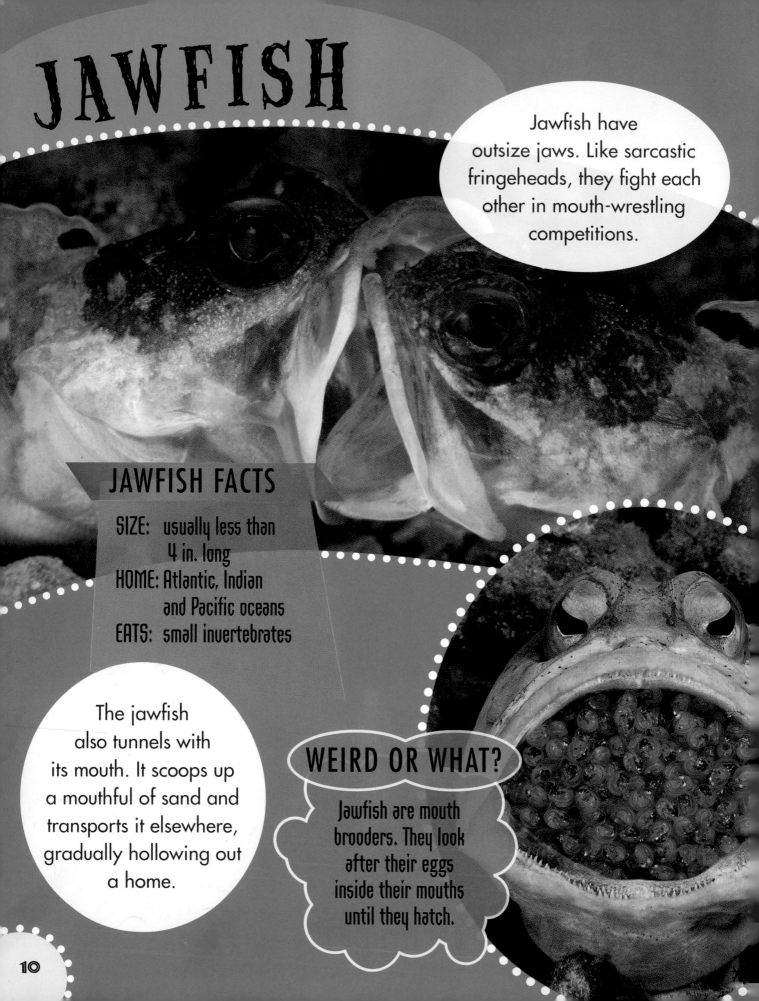

JAWFISH

Jawfish have outsize jaws. Like sarcastic fringeheads, they fight each other in mouth-wrestling competitions.

JAWFISH FACTS

SIZE: usually less than 4 in. long
HOME: Atlantic, Indian and Pacific oceans
EATS: small invertebrates

The jawfish also tunnels with its mouth. It scoops up a mouthful of sand and transports it elsewhere, gradually hollowing out a home.

WEIRD OR WHAT?

Jawfish are mouth brooders. They look after their eggs inside their mouths until they hatch.

Leafy Sea Dragon

Now you see it; now you don't. The leafy sea dragon is named for the flaps of skin all over its body that look just like seaweed. They provide brilliant camouflage!

WEIRD OR WHAT?

Female sea dragons lay their eggs in a pouch on the male's tail. He looks after them until they hatch.

LEAFY SEA DRAGON FACTS

SIZE: up to 9 in. long
HOME: off the coast of Australia
EATS: shrimps, sea lice, fish fry

Sea dragons are relatives of sea horses. They have a mouth like a drinking straw for sucking up tiny shrimps.

LIONFISH

Lionfish live in coral reefs. They're named for their impressive "mane" of stripy spines.

LIONFISH FACTS

SIZE: around 12 in. long
HOME: the Pacific Ocean, but they've recently spread to the Caribbean and Mediterranean
EATS: small fish, crustaceans

These spines may look pretty, but they're very dangerous. Each one is coated in venomous mucus. You wouldn't want to step on one of these while swimming!

WEIRD OR WHAT?

Lionfish are pests in parts of the Caribbean. They prey on native fish and have no natural predators. Fishermen who catch them and hand them in are paid a reward!

Lionfish sometimes herd their fish or shrimp prey into a corner before starting to eat.

PARROTFISH

Parrotfish change color at different stages in their development. Most parrotfish start out female and later change into males. Imagine that!

This fish has a beak like a parrot, but it can't talk! Parrotfish use their beaks to scrape algae off rocks and corals.

PARROTFISH FACTS

SIZE: usually 12-20 in. long (some species top 3 ft.)

HOME: tropical and subtropical shallows worldwide

EATS: algae, coral polyps

WEIRD OR WHAT?

Some parrotfish wear pajamas! At night they wrap up their body in a coating of mucus. Scientists think it makes them more difficult for eels and other hunters to sniff out.

PUFFERFISH

BEFORE

Pufferfish can puff up like a balloon. This defense makes them too much of a mouthful for most predators—especially since many species are covered in prickles. They're poisonous, too!

PUFFERFISH FACTS

SIZE: up to 36 in. long (but the smallest species is just 1 in.)
HOME: usually tropical waters
EATS: algae, invertebrates (e.g. sponges, sea urchins)

AFTER

WEIRD OR WHAT?

In Japan the poisonous flesh of the pufferfish— fugu—is a delicacy. Only trained chefs can prepare it.

Pufferfish rely on sight to find their food. They can move each eye independently.

OCEAN SUNFISH

The ocean sunfish is no beauty, but it is the world's heaviest bony fish. It starts life measuring just a fraction of an inch, but eventually weighs about a ton.

WEIRD OR WHAT?

Ocean sunfish females produce more eggs than any other vertebrate—as many as 300 million at a time! How would you like that many brothers and sisters?

OCEAN SUNFISH FACTS

SIZE: usually up to 5 ft.
HOME: open ocean, tropical to temperate waters
EATS: jellyfish, fish, crustaceans

The sunfish is named for its habit of "sunbathing" at the surface. It may do this to encourage seagulls, which land and pick off parasites!

OARFISH

The four species of oarfish are true "monsters of the deep." This giant oarfish is the world's longest bony fish. It usually grows to about 30 feet, but there are reports of sightings of fish nearly twice that length.

WEIRD OR WHAT?

Myths about sea serpents might be based on sightings of oarfish.

Oarfish spend most of their time in deep water. They sometimes swim in an upright pose.

OARFISH FACTS

SIZE: usually 30 ft. long
HOME: deep waters of tropical and subtropical seas
EATS: zooplankton (e.g. tiny crustaceans), jellyfish, squid, small fish

PELICAN EEL

PELICAN EEL FACTS

SIZE: about 3 ft. long
HOME: deep waters of tropical and subtropical seas
EATS: small crustaceans

The pelican eel is a deep-sea weirdo. It's named for its elastic mouth, which resembles a pelican bird's stretchy throat.

WEIRD OR WHAT?

The pelican eel produces red flashing lights from its tail, probably to attract prey in the gloomy deep where it lives.

The fish's gaping mouth is about 10 inches long. The rest of its body is snakelike.

Most fish soon die if they are taken out of the water—but not the mudskipper. It can breathe on land as well as under water.

MUDSKIPPER FACTS

SIZE: up to 12 in. long
HOME: tropical swamps and estuaries around the Indo-Pacific
EATS: small crustaceans

WEIRD OR WHAT?

Mudskippers take in oxygen from the air through their skin. They also save bubbles of air in their gills.

MUDSKIPPER

Mudskippers live in coastal regions. When the tide goes out, they walk or skip around the mud flats looking for food.

WEIRD OR WHAT?

Coelacanth eggs develop inside the mother's body, perhaps for as long as three years. Then the mother gives birth to about five well-developed young.

COELACANTH

For a long time scientists only knew about the coelacanth from fossils. This fossil from Germany is 150 million years old.

COELACANTH FACTS

SIZE: around 5 ft. long
HOME: deep waters of the Indo-Pacific
EATS: fish, squid

Scientists thought coelacanths had become extinct millions of years ago. But then, in 1938, a live coelacanth was caught!

19

SWORDFISH, MARLIN, AND SAILFISH

Marlins, swordfish, and sailfish are three of the fastest hunters in the ocean. They can power through the water at speeds of about 65 miles per hour.

WEIRD OR WHAT?

The sailfish can change color depending on its mood.

sailfish

This sailfish is feeding on sardines.

SAILFISH FACTS

SIZE: up to 12 ft.
HOME: warm and temperate waters worldwide
EATS: fish

swordfish

These fish hunt by sight. Marlins and swordfish even have a special organ next to their eyes that heats their eyes and brain, helping them to see better.

SWORDFISH FACTS

SIZE: up to 15 ft.
HOME: warm and temperate waters worldwide
EATS: squid, fish

Game fishermen like the challenge of trying to catch marlins. Luckily, this one might just get away!

marlin

MARLIN FACTS

SIZE: up to 20 ft.
HOME: warm and temperate waters worldwide
EATS: fish

BASKING SHARK

BASKING SHARK FACTS

SIZE: up to 46 ft. long
HOME: temperate waters
of the Atlantic, Pacific,
and Indian oceans
EATS: zooplankton

With its gigantic, gaping mouth, the basking shark is a terrifying sight! However, this shark is a gentle giant, feeding on tiny zooplankton.

The basking shark is a filter feeder. When it closes its mouth, it forces water out through its gills. The gill rakers sieve out any plankton prey.

WEIRD OR WHAT?

Only one other fish is larger than the basking shark—the whale shark.

gill raker

HAMMERHEAD SHARK

Hammerheads have to be the strangest-looking sharks!

Having their eyes at the tips of the hammerhead gives the sharks excellent all-round vision.

HAMMERHEAD SHARK FACTS

SIZE: 3-20 ft. depending on species
HOME: temperate and tropical waters worldwide
EATS: fish (e.g. rays), crustaceans

WEIRD OR WHAT?

Scalloped hammerheads are the only sharks to form schools. As many as 500 may swim together!

23

ARCHER FISH

No fish can match the archer fish at target practice!

WEIRD OR WHAT?

The archer fish can hit prey from a distance of 5 feet.

When the fish spots a creepy-crawly on an overhanging plant, it shoots a jet of "spit" at it. Gotcha! The prey falls into the water and is gobbled up by the fish.

ARCHER FISH FACTS

SIZE: 2-4 in. (but one species grows up to 16 in. long)
HOME: fresh and coastal waters around the Indo Pacific
EATS: insects, spiders

FLYING FISH

Is it a bird or a fish? Flying fish have a neat trick for escaping marine predators—they leave the water! Swimming at top speed, the fish can break through the surface and glide through the air.

FLYING FISH FACTS

SIZE: up to 18 in. long
HOME: tropical and subtropical waters worldwide
EATS: plankton

WEIRD OR WHAT?

A flying fish can cover a distance of 600 ft. in a single glide.

The fish glide on stiff, outstretched pectoral fins. Their average gliding speed is about 10 miles per hour.

CLEANER WRASSE

Fish can't brush their teeth, as you can. Instead, they use cleaner wrasse. Cleaner wrasse are the trash collectors of the coral reef.

WEIRD OR WHAT?

A cleaner wrasse can clean around 50 fish an hour.

Look closely inside this gray reef shark's mouth—a fearless cleaner wrasse is cleaning its teeth!

CLEANER WRASSE FACTS

SIZE: up to 8 in. long
HOME: tropical reefs
EATS: parasites, dead skin

Cleaner wrasse feed on parasites and dead skin. Fish that need cleaning recognize the wrasse by their stripy bodies.

They are also attracted by a special dance that the wrasse perform—spreading out their tail fins and waving their bottoms up and down! Reef fish will even line up to take their turn with a cleaner wrasse.

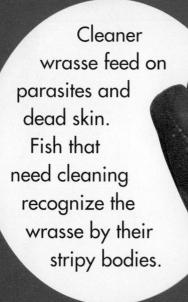

This moray eel is at a wrasse "cleaning station." Three wrasse and two cleaner shrimps are giving its skin a spring clean.

FANGTOOTH

This fish looks like a monster from outer space! The fangtooth is one of the fiercest-looking fish in the ocean, thanks to its long, needle-sharp teeth. It lives in the deepest parts of the ocean.

WEIRD OR WHAT?

When it shuts its mouth, the fangtooth houses its longest lower fangs in two special sockets on either side of its brain.

FANGTOOTH FACTS

SIZE: up to 7 in.
HOME: deep waters worldwide
EATS: anything that passes by

This fangtooth baby, or larva, has protective spines to deter predators.

ANGLERFISH

All anglerfish have a lure that dangles above their face, tempting prey to come near. The deep-sea anglerfish's lure glows in the dark, so it can be seen through the gloom.

lure

WEIRD OR WHAT?

Some male anglerfish live like parasites on the body of a much-bigger female. She may carry as many as six at a time.

ANGLERFISH FACTS

SIZE: females up to 7 in., males less that 1 in.
HOME: deep waters worldwide
EATS: small fish, crustaceans

GLOSSARY

alga (plural algae) One of a group of living things that include seaweeds and some plankton.

antivenin A chemical that can stop the effects of venom, such as paralysis.

camouflage Colors or patterns that help an animal to blend in to the surrounding environment to avoid being seen by predators, prey or both.

coral A tiny marine animal related to sea anemones. Its soft body, known as a polyp, has a circle of tentacles.

crustacean An animal with two-parted legs and a segmented body covered by a hard outer skeleton (an exoskeleton). Crabs and shrimps are crustaceans.

fry Newly hatched fish.

gill The organ that allows fish and some other underwater animals to breathe.

inedible Describes something that cannot be eaten or is not good to eat.

invertebrate An animal that has no backbone. Some invertebrates, such as crabs, protect their bodies with a hard outer skeleton, called an exoskeleton. Others, such as jellyfish, have soft bodies.

lure Something that is used to tempt—for example, to bring prey animals near.

modified Altered or changed.

mollusk A soft-bodied animal with no backbone and, often, a shell. Snails and mussels are mollusks.

mucus A slimy substance that an animal secretes.

parasite A living thing that does not produce or find its own food, but instead lives on a host that it relies on for food.

pectoral fin One of the pair of fins on either side of a fish's head.

plankton Microscopic plants, algae, and animals that float in the oceans. Animal plankton is known as zooplankton.

predator An animal that hunts and kills other animals for food.

prey An animal that is hunted and killed by another animal for food.

reef A stony structure that forms in warm, shallow waters, built from the old exoskeletons of tiny corals.

spawning Laying eggs.

species One particular type of living thing. Members of the same species look similar and can reproduce together in the wild.

subtropical Describes the regions of the earth that lie between tropical and temperate areas.

temperate Describes the two regions of the earth that lie between the tropics and the poles, where the climate is warm in summer and cool in winter.

tentacle A slender, flexible organ used to sense, grab, or move around.

territory The area that an animal defends against other animals, usually of the same species.

trawler A fishing boat that catches fish and other sea creatures by dragging a net over the seabed.

tropical Describes the warm part of the world near the equator (the imaginary line that circles the middle of the earth).

venom A chemical that is injected into another animal to paralyze it.

vertebrate An animal that has a backbone.

FURTHER INFORMATION

Books
Classifying Animals: Fish by Sarah Wilkes (World Almanac Library, 2009)

The Deep, Deep Ocean by John Woodward (Brown Bear, 2010)

Diving to a Deep Sea Volcano by Kenneth Mallory (Houghton Mifflin, 2006)

Eye Wonder: Ocean by Mary Ling and Sue Thornton (Dorling Kindersley, 2004)

Nature's Monsters: Weird and Wonderful Fish by Gerrie McCall (Gareth Stevens Publishing, 2005)

DVDs
The Blue Planet (BBC Warner, 2001)

IMAX: Under the Sea (IMAX, 2010)

Web Sites
BBC Wildlife Finder
www.bbc.co.uk/nature/animals

Dive Gallery: Leafy Sea Dragon
www.divegallery.com/Leafy_Sea_Dragon

National Geographic: Fish
http://animals.nationalgeographic.com/
animals/fish.html

Woods Hole Oceanographic Institution
www.whoi.edu

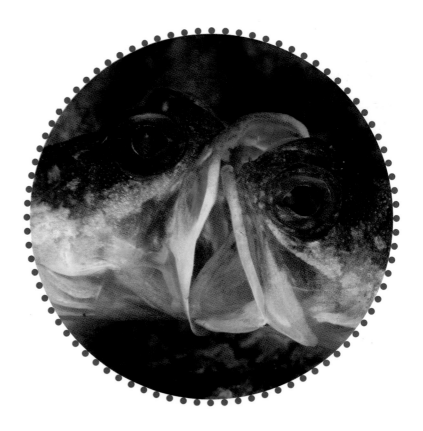

INDEX

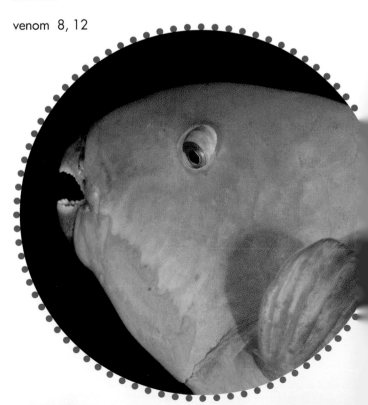